Guide To MYNAHS

by

Robert L. Busenbark

and

Henry J. Bates

Distributed in the U.S.A. by T.F.H. Publications, Inc., 211 West Sylvania Avenue, P.O. Box 27, Neptune City, N.J. 07753; in England by T.F.H. (Gt. Britain) Ltd., 13 Nutley Lane, Reigate, Surrey; in Canada to the book store and library trade by Clarke, Irwin & Company, Clarwin House, 791 St. Clair Avenue West, Toronto 10, Ontario; in Canada to the pet trade by Rolf C. Hagen Ltd., 3225 Sartelon Street, Montreal 382, Quebec; in Southeast Asia by Y.W. Ong, 9 Lorong 36 Geylang, Singapore 14; in Australia and the south Pacific by Pet Imports Pty. Ltd., P.O. Box 149, Brookvale 2100, N.S.W., Australia. Published by T.F.H. Publications Inc. Ltd., The British Crown Colony of Hong Kong.

Cover photo and most text photos by
Sam Fehrenz

ISBN 0-87666-425-7

Contents

HENRY J. BATES

Henry J. Bates, has been a bird and pet fancier for practically all his life. His interests centered around birds and tropical fish during his high school years. Following service in the Air Corps, Hank attended Fresno State College and resumed his hobbies of collecting and breeding tropical fish and birds. Graduating from Fresno State in 1950, Hank and Bob were so deeply involved in their mutual hobby of raising birds that they decided to go into business. In addition to the collection of birds at the Palos Verdes Bird Farm, Bob and Hank each have private collections in their homes for enjoyment, observation, and breeding.

ROBERT L. BUSENBARK

Robert L. Busenbark is called Bob by everyone who knows him. His interest and experience in pets, interrupted only by service in the Air Corps, closely parallels that of Hank. Bob is particularly adept at taming and training difficult birds of the parrot family and has developed some unusual and successful techniques which are described in this book. The Palos Verdes Bird Farm in Walteria, California, was opened by Hank and Bob in the fall of 1952. Gradually building their business, Hank and Bob added appreciably to their store of knowledge and experience by constantly working with birds of the parrot family, with finches, and with softbilled birds.

Chapter 1

Introduction

Mynah birds are not only the greatest of all the talking birds, but they also make excellent tame pets. One reason for their reliability as pets is the painstaking and thorough way youngsters are handreared and completely tamed before they are shipped from their native lands. In pet shops the mynah season usually begins late in April or early in May and ends about September. Most seasons vary somewhat, and importers try to import enough birds near the end of the season to supply the Christmas markets as well. This is often not possible, and so summer or early fall is the best time to shop for your pet mynah. Also, birds available at these periods are younger, more easily trained, and usually lower in price. You should obtain your mynah before it is six months of age in order to develop its maximum potential with minimum effort. Don't worry about your investment in any case because mynahs given proper care and diet can live for twenty-five years.

Youngsters up to six or eight months of age are never very attractive when compared to most other cage birds, but they have enough talent to outshine their lack of colors and rather ordinary shape. In fact, their remarkable ability to imitate the human voice in all its different inflections with amazing fidelity have helped to make the mynah one of the most popular bird pets in the world. Both sexes are equally talented.

Altogether, there are ten subspecies of *Gracula religiosa* spread over a large area from India through Southeast Asia, Indonesia, and the Philippines. Their great growth in popularity since World War II

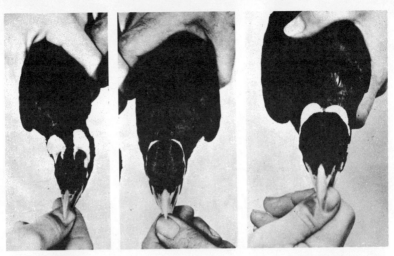

Left to right: Lesser Hill Mynah, Assam Greater Indian Hill Mynah, Javan Hill Mynah. Note the large lappets on the Lesser as contrasted to the small lappets on the Assam, a much larger bird. The Javan is the largest of the three birds but has a medium size lappet.

is probably due to the influence of returning servicemen from the Orient. Many of the subspecies show remarkable variations. All three of the best known forms are subspecies, and are therefore very closely related.

GREATER INDIA HILL MYNAH

The Greater India Hill Mynah is the subspecies *Gracula religiosa intermedia*. It occurs in a long area of northeastern India in the foothills of the Himalayas, Nepal, Burma, Thailand, and several other points including parts of Vietnam, Laos, Cambodia, and southern China.

A few years ago when all the mynahs for pets were imported from India, considerable attention was given to two different varieties of Greater India Hill Mynah: the Assam and the Nepal varieties. Actually, one race inhabits both areas; and the difference in appearance is very slight if any. Any differences which might occur in talents were probably due to the different methods of caring for the youngsters before export. Methods of "harvesting" youngsters as well as age of the birds when removed from the nest for handfeeding vary from area to area, and this can make a very noticeable difference in tameness, stamina, and appearance.

RACES OF TALKING MYNAHS

A map of mynahs: This sketch by Dr. W. C. Dilger of Cornell University illustrates the two species and the several subspecies of talking mynahs. The important ones in the pet trade are **A, B, C, G,** and **I.** They are: (A) Lesser India Hill Mynah **(Gracula religiosa indica)**; (B) Greater India Hill Mynah **(Gracula religiosa peninsularis)**; (C) Greater India Hill Mynah **(Gracula religiosa intermedia)**; (D) Philippine Talking Mynah **(Gracula religiosa palawanensis)**; (E) Ceylon Mynah **(Gracula ptilogenys)**; (F) Andaman or Nicobar Mynah **(Gracula religiosa andamanensis)**; (G) Nias Island or Giant Mynah, also called Java Hill Mynah **(Gracula religiosa robusta)**; (H) Java Hill Mynah, so called **(Gracula religiosa batuensis)**; (I) Java Hill Mynah **(Gracula religiosa religiosa)**; (J) Java Hill Mynah, so-called **(Gracula religiosa venerata)**; (K) Java Hill Mynah, so-called **(Gracula religiosa mertensi)**.

AVERAGE
LENGTH   305 m.m
WING   165 mm
BILL   24 m.m.

Gracula religiosa intermedia Greater India Hill Mynah

The Greater India Hill Mynah is now exported to the worldwide pet trade from Thailand as well as from India.

The total size is about eleven inches including the squared tail of three and a half inches. Adults have glossy black plumage with reflections of green, blue, and purple iridescence. Head feathers are short with a velvety texture. Youngsters have dull black plumage with no lustrous shadings. The feet and legs are yellow, and the beak of adults is bright orange fading to yellow on the tip. Youngsters lack the bright orange coloring on the beaks showing instead a paler shade of yellow-orange. A large band of white occurs across the central area of the flight feathers.

Wattles are bare fleshy skin areas. There are many wattle variations within the subspecies which occur with age.

In youngsters, the wattle skin is taut, underdeveloped, and ivory in color. In adulthood, the wattle skin is bright yellow; and two loose flaps of wattle flesh develop slowly. At about a year of age, they are only slight bulbous swellings. Males grow longer flaps than do females.

The wattle skin has a broad starting area below the eyes down to a point even with the lowest point of the lower mandible. It extends backward over most of the lower facial area and becomes narrower on the nape, but the two sides do not quite meet. A small triangle of black feathers interrupts the fleshy area behind and below the eyes.

A second Indian subspecies, *peninsularis*, is found in the foothills of the northeastern peninsular area which is considerably more southerly than the above race. These are about an inch smaller, and their nape flaps are less broad than in the above mentioned race. The triangle of black feathers is less triangular because the opening behind the eye is much broader. The beak is also smaller and more slender.

This front and rear view photograph shows the full wattle pattern of a young adult. The wattles are close but do not quite meet on the nape of the Greater India Hill or the Java Hill Mynahs. In the less talented Lesser India Hill Mynah, the wattles are broadly separated with the ends turned forward towards the crown.

This race, sometimes erroneously called the Assam variety, is also correctly called the Greater India Hill Mynah; and most people will not be aware of the differences. Some of those who are aware of the differences feel that this race is less talented than the *intermedia*, but this opinion is not totally justified.

LESSER INDIA HILL MYNAH *(Gracula religiosa indica)*

The Lesser India Hill Mynah from southwestern India and Ceylon is now seldom available. It was once imported in large numbers as a low priced substitute for the Greater India Hill Mynah when the latter was an expensive bird. It was never considered a satisfactory pet because most were too old when they were exported. Most of them were untameable, and they rarely learned to talk.

These two pictures above, and right, illustrate the differences in wattle patterns to be found in some of the subspecies birds being sold as Java Hill Mynahs. Five subspecies are sold as Java Hill Mynahs. Size is actually more important than native origin.

A good part of the disappointment stems from the collecting methods. The youngsters when taken are older than the Greater India Hill Mynahs which are handreared for the pet trade. If they were hand fed in India at all, it was for too short a period to instill complete tameness; but even when taken early and fed by hand, the Lesser India Hill Mynah cannot compare favorably with the Greater India Hill Mynah in talking ability or in its steadiness as a tame pet.

This species is about nine and a half inches long. It is noticeably smaller and more slender than the Greater India Hill Mynah. The beak is far more slender, and the head is smaller. The wattles are the most distinguishing features. A wide separation occurs between the wattles on the nape. Instead of nearly meeting, they turn forward

up to the crown showing two bold U-shaped figures when viewed from the top. Adults show notched ridges on the inner areas. The triangle of black feathers is absent, but in its place is a feathered area which totally separates a small area of wattled flesh below the eyes. The flaps on the nape develop slowly as do those of the Greater India Hill Mynah.

Java Hill Mynah in center is noticeably larger than the Greater India Hill Mynahs on both sides. Also distinctive are the differences in the pattern of the wattle below and behind the eyes. Photographed at about a year of age, the wattle flaps on the nape are just starting to grow.

JAVA HILL MYNAH (*Gracula religiosa religiosa*)

As far as the pet trade is concerned, the rare Java Hill Mynah is the king of the mynahs. It is considerably more expensive than the Greater India Hill Mynah. It is noticeably larger than the Indian varieties in all ways especially in the head and the thick beak, but in actual length it is only an inch longer.

14

AVERAGE
LENGTH   255 m.m.
WING   140 m.m.
BILL   24 m.m.

Gracula religiosa indica Lesser India Hill Mynah

AVERAGE
LENGTH   260 m.m.
WING   152 m.m.
BILL   23 m.m.

Gracula ptilogenys Ceylon Mynah

The loose wattle flaps on the nape grow extensively after the bird is a year old although the starting age for this development is variable. The age of this bird can be estimated as being at least fifteen to eighteen months of age. Wattle flaps on females are smaller than those of males. Birds in aviaries as a general rule usually develop larger flaps than do caged birds.

The wattle skin in the lower facial area is less extensive than in the Greater India Hill Mynah, and the feathered area below and behind the eye divides the wattle. In some races, the division is not complete. The flaps of wattle skin on the nape are larger in adulthood than those of the Greater India Hill Mynah.

This subspecies occurs in Malaysia, Borneo, and many Indonesian islands. The popular name is therefore a little misleading. It is now rarely available on a consistent basis to the pet trade. When regular channels of distribution or methods of collecting have been interrupted as has happened with this race, there is a danger that many of those which are imported will be too old to be satisfactory talking pets. This has happened with the Java Hill Mynah. Some of the Java Hill Mynahs owned by the writers have been the best talkers they have known. Others, too old to learn, have been disappointments.

The Java Hill Mynah has an even better potential as a talker than the Greater India Hill Mynah. They speak very clearly if well taught, and seem to be more adept at learning to speak in lower voice registers. Except for the precaution regarding age mentioned above, the Java Hill Mynah is highly recommended.

There are three other Indonesian subspecies with slight differences in size and wattled areas. If these become available to the pet trade (which is possible but not at present probable) they will undoubtedly be represented as Java Hill Mynahs. These subspecies named *batuensis*, *venerata*, and *mertensi* are island dwellers and therefore isolated from each other.

Another subspecies, the Nias Island Mynah (*Gracula religiosa robusta*), is the giant of the mynahs. It occurs in four West Sumatran Islands, and has in the past been available on a very occasional basis. It has also been erroneously called the Java Hill Mynah in the trade. It is larger than the other birds called Java Hill Mynahs and has a more majestic demeanor and appearance.

The size totals about fifteen inches in length. The head is larger, and the beak is thicker. The piece of wattle skin below the eye is very limited in proportion to other characteristics. It is longer but far more slender, and the separation from the nape is considerably greater.

Youngsters become excellent talkers and are better than the real Java Hill Mynah. After seeing these birds, most people are somewhat disappointed in the other subspecies which are properly called Java Hill Mynahs.

The Philippine Talking Mynah (*Gracula religiosa palawanensis*) is a slightly smaller version of the Java Hill Mynah. It occurs in the Palawan area and neighboring small islands of the Philippines. It is about eleven inches long, which is about the same as the Greater India Hill Mynah. However, the larger head, thicker beak, and wattle pattern are more like those of the Java Hill Mynah. The flaps on the nape are smaller.

This race is popular as a pet in the Philippines, but it is not very often exported. Youngsters are not harvested or handreared in sufficient quantities to market abroad, and so most people in the industry do not regard this race as a good talker. This misconception is due to the fact that most of the few which have been exported were too old to learn very much. The point of diminishing returns had already been reached. The authors have owned a few of these birds which became very good talkers.

Still another race of the Hill Mynah is *Gracula religiosa andamanensis* from the Nicobar and Andaman Islands. This race is like the Greater India Hill Mynah in size and all other respects except the beak which is thicker. It does not reach worldwide export markets and therefore is not known in the pet trade.

The only other species in this genus is the Ceylon Mynah (*Gracula ptilogenys*) which is popular as a pet in Ceylon. However, it is not exported to the pet markets. This species is slightly heavier than the Lesser India Hill Mynah, but the length is approximately the same. The only wattled area is the flaps on the nape. The coloring of the beak is red-orange with a broad area of black at the base.

The entire mynah family is a very large one. It includes starlings and many birds of similar size and characteristics some of which are arbitrarily called by both popular names of starling, and mynah. Members are spread in most areas of the world, and the introduction of some members into areas out of their native ranges has caused many problems. These will be discussed later.

The smaller mynahs and starlings have bold swaggering walking habits seeming always to be taking giant strides. The Hill Mynahs and a few others among the larger birds do not walk but hop when they are on the ground. In the wild state, the Hill Mynahs are forest birds which seldom descend to the ground.

Other types of birds also learn to talk to a lesser extent than mynahs. These include crows, ravens, and even some magpies. None have talents to approach those of the mynahs. There is an old outdated and untrue, but stubbornly persistent belief that crows and ravens will talk only if their tongues have been split. This absurd and cruel treatment can never be justified, and it certainly is not necessary.

The nape wattles of the older bird at the top are longer and are already in an advanced stage of development compared to the bird in the center. Note the variation of the division in the wattle behind the eye. This is relatively common in some of the various subspecies which are called Java Hill Mynahs.

The Purple Glossy Grackle, a cousin of the Mynah, is kept as a cage bird by European fanciers. It is not a talker. Photo by Lacey.

Chapter 2
Habits and Care

Mynahs have very alert personalities, and youngsters learn quickly. They respond strongly to proper handling and training, as well as to adverse treatment. With gentle handling, the total tameness of newly imported youngsters will develop them into affectionate, friendly adults. Erratic handling by the owner, reluctance to develop a companionship, sudden movements, and slapping at the cage as a means of punishment, instill a wildness which leads to dangerous panics. Such treatment destroys all pet potential in the carefully handreared youngster. Never tease a mynah; it will quickly learn to retaliate.

It is important that you start proper procedures as soon as you acquire your new mynah. Diet, training, and speech lessons are outlined in their respective chapters. It is far easier to develop good methods of care and training in the beginning than to correct errors after they have become entrenched.

BATHING

Daily bathing is very important to mynahs. Bathing helps a mynah to attain a sleek and well groomed appearance, and it is obvious that the bird thoroughly enjoys the ritual. As soon as your young mynah settles down to its new environment, you can establish a routine for regular bathing. Morning bathing is best. Evening bathing is dangerous because the bird may not dry completely before it goes to sleep, and this could lead to colds and sickness. Morning bathing can become an easily learned, regular habit. The best time to offer the bath is about an hour before you clean the cage so that all the spattered

Daily bathing is very beneficial to mynahs, and they thoroughly enjoy it. Contemplation at this stage is usually very short.

Thigh deep and still looking a little undecided or perhaps testing the temperature, the bird in this second stage of the bath also usually makes a quick decision.

The third stage of the bath is very active and is accompanied by vigorous long range splashing. For this reason, it is better to set a regular routine for bathing to be completed before the cage is cleaned. In this way, splashed water can be wiped dry.

The shaking off surplus water stage is followed by meticulous and complicated grooming. Frequent bathing helps to maintain the high gloss and good grooming which mynahs like.

Mynahs can be sprayed for mites as a periodic precaution. The cage should be sprayed also. Mites usually do not become much of a problem with mynahs because their cages are given frequent thorough scrubbings.

water can be wiped dry. It is a good idea to remove the tray and place the cage over a piece of easily cleaned plastic. This reduces the chance of rusting and your cage will last longer.

Your pet shop will have many suitable bathing dishes to fit your mynah's cage. Choose one that will hold a water depth of about two inches.

NIGHT SHELTERS

Young mynahs have a natural tendency to roost inside a small shelter. Many people give their birds a paper sack at night, and the birds quite readily take to this type of night shelter. Although this is not really necessary, many people continue the practice into adulthood. The birds seem to like the extra seclusion, and they possibly gain an extra sense of security. If their cage is placed in an area where there would be a tendency to disturb the birds late at night, the paper sack is a very good idea. The idea of extra safety for the bird is largely a misconception. It is true that birds roosting in sacks will have less chance of being in drafts, but the cages of any birds should not be in drafts at any time.

TOYS

Mynahs often enjoy toys, but there are not many which can be considered suitable. They must not be small enough to be swallowed or of a texture that will allow the birds to become entangled and injured. Among the best toys for mynahs are bells like those given to parrots, ping pong balls, or similarly sized balls such as are given to parrakeets.

Young mynahs have an amusing preference for roosting in paper bags at night. This can be beneficial since it gives greater seclusion from late lights. It is also a further safeguard against drafts.

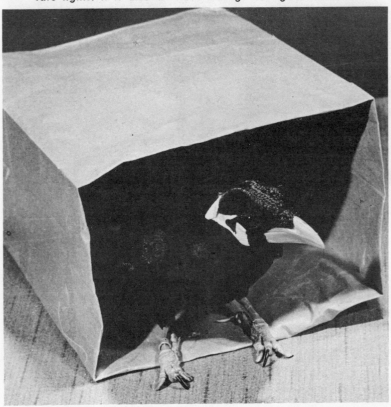

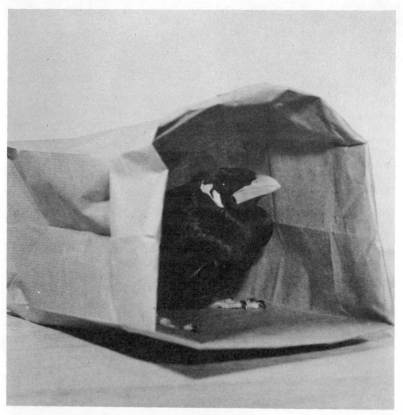

The squat posture of this Mynah does not indicate disease. It is simply a young bird settling down for a snooze.

CAGE FREE PETS

Mynahs are excellent as tame pets, and all pet birds should be given some time out of their cages for exercise as well as for companionship. Because of their droppings, this should be allowed only in a room where soilage can be easily cleaned. Also, you should wear old clothes which cannot be harmed by droppings.

WING CLIPPING

In order to restrict the movement of a bird which is allowed out of its cage, it is wise to clip wing feathers. There are two methods of doing this. The first is to clip the flight feathers on one wing. They should *not* be clipped short. Short shafts are liable to split or become frayed down into the feather follicle, and this could cause ingrown feathers when the new ones start to grow. It is best to clip half to two-thirds of the total length of the flights. The authors prefer to clip the feathers on one wing, but many people prefer to clip both

Tame mynahs which are frequently removed from their cages should have their wings clipped. Clipped wings are also useful in taming or retraining. However, this bird's wings are being clipped too short for safety. The frayed flight feathers already indicate that this bird is apparently subject to periods of fright during which it damages the feathers by beating its wings against cage bars. Clipping the flights this short could result in split feather shafts during such activity, and this may result in ingrown feathers when new ones grow. It would be better to "strip the flights" on this bird or to cut at the lower boundaries of the white wing bar.

wings. This is a matter of personal preference. Some people do not like the unbalanced appearance one clipped wing gives. The authors prefer one clipped wing because the unbalanced flight discourages frequent attempts to fly. Other fanciers prefer to leave the outer three feathers intact.

The other method of clipping or stripping the wings is to trim the webs from the feather shaft leaving the shafts intact with perhaps the web also intact on the outer tips. Many youngsters arriving from India already have their wings clipped in this manner. Those arriving from Thailand rarely have clipped wings.

An occasional feather is replaced during non-moulting seasons, but most replacements will occur during the moulting season. Feathers which have grown out will need to be clipped again, but they should never be clipped while they are in the pinfeather stage because they will bleed profusely during this period of development. Should this happen, the chapter on ailments will teach you how to stop the bleeding.

SUNSHINE

Sunshine can be very dangerous to mynahs. Many people are accustomed to putting their pet birds out for a sunbath, but mynahs are deep-forest-dwelling birds. Sunshine is quite foreign to them. They can take only very short periods of exposure to sun without harm. In aviaries they can retreat to shady areas in sunny weather. When they are restricted to cages which are placed in the sun, there is no chance for a shady retreat. Many mynahs have been accidentally killed in this manner. They usually suffer severe convulsions at first. For treatment, see the chapter on diseases and ailments.

TEMPERATURES

Mynahs are usually very hardy. Most of the older literature states that they cannot be subjected to temperatures lower than fifty degrees, Fahrenheit. This is not quite true, but it is a good safeguard. Mynahs kept indoors at all times become restricted to very limited temperature variations. They become somewhat like hothouse plants. Under prolonged pampering, cold or hot extremes can cause severe problems. Under such conditions, mynahs become easily vulnerable to colds and pneumonia.

Mynahs become sturdier if they become accustomed to a latitude of temperatures, although they should never be subjected to real extremes. Symptoms for hot weather distress are panting and reduced activity. Cold weather distress signs are fluffed plumage, shrinking wattles, and faded or bluish shaded wattles.

In many moderate climates in the United States, mynahs are safely wintered out of doors in regular aviaries with wired open flights and covered shelters which eliminate drafts. Under these conditions the birds become very strong and resistant to most ailments. They are prepared for the outdoors by starting them outside during the summer so that they can gradually become accustomed to lower temperatures.

In the Southern California aviaries of the authors, many mynahs have wintered outdoors year after year with no problems. Temperatures are moderate to be sure, but they frequently are below forty degrees Fahrenheit and occasionally below thirty degrees during the colder periods. They should perhaps not be subjected to any extremes below these levels. The authors have no information regarding outdoor wintering of mynahs in the colder zones of the United States or in England. Even if it has been accomplished, it would certainly be risky.

Chapter 3

What Happens to Your Bird Before You Get It

Captive mynahs are not bred commercially. To supply the world markets with top quality youngsters at reasonable prices, a thriving efficient industry has developed in Thailand. The baby mynah industry first started in India and soon spread to Thailand where mynahs are common in the northern part of the country.

The authors have imported from both countries and have observed the care routine of the youngsters in Thailand before shipment to world markets. It is an interesting process.

Collectors put their mark on the trees where they have located a nest of youngsters. They estimate the time so that they can take the youngsters from three weeks of age to a few days before they leave the nest. This is the perfect age range for the pet market because the youngsters are robust and easily hand fed. They very quickly become totally tame. The pliable personalities have no bad habits. The youngsters quickly adapt to their new environment and clamor constantly for human attention.

The baby mynahs are transferred to the domestic diet available in Thailand in an amazingly short time because they are all fed by hand. The diet is mainly boiled rice, diced fish, and a cooked green vegetable which is popular with the Thai people. There are other items added to this mixture to round out the diet. The most unusual additive is very hot peppers. The birds love them.

The people of Thailand enjoy very highly spiced foods; and they use hot peppers abundantly in their own foods. Mynahs thrive on them, and they are considered to be a very important part of the diet.

The youngsters are kept in large groups in long, broad wire cages. The wire bottoms permit their copious droppings to pass through the cage onto the concrete below. Frequent washing of the concrete does not disturb the birds.

Attendants usually care for several hundred birds. When not cleaning cages or concrete they are usually feeding the youngsters, which must happen several times a day. These frequent feedings are chaotic affairs with all the babies crowding near. The attendant faces a sea of gaping mouths and the raucous squeals of ever-hungry growing fledglings. They clamber up his arms and perch on his shoulders, hands, and head. At this age, they would not consider picking up food themselves. They want to have it placed in their mouths, and they give distinct and frantic impressions that beyond the gaping mouths are bottomless pits which will never be filled.

With so many youngsters crowding around and jockeying for the most favorable positions, it seems impossible for attendants to know which have been fed and which ones still need food. Gradually as the bottomless pits do become filled, the birds quiet down, close their mouths, and drift away from food and attendant. The attendant watches closely for any listless stragglers or those uninterested in food because this would be an indication of a weakness or illness. Special attention and separation are given to any falling into this category; but, with such care as this, there are seldom any problems.

By the time shipping age of six weeks is reached, the birds know how to pick up their own food and do not require any special handling in transit. They are packed in long, broad crates about six or eight inches high. The crates have wired, sloped sides so that they can be stacked one on top of another without blocking off the air supply. The rest of the crates are enclosed to protect the birds from drafts. Usually it is reasonably dark inside so that the birds do not move around unnecessarily. Baby mynahs do not panic in transit; and, with air travel greatly improved, they reach their destinations quickly and safely. Usually each crate accommodates about twenty-five youngsters.

The authors have not witnessed mynah care in India, but the mynah birds they have imported from that country arrive in much the same condition. The food is different in shipments from India, however. It seems to be composed solely of finely ground gram powder generously moistened.

When shipments arrive, importers are kept especially busy for several days. They must handfeed all the birds several times a day. Although the babies have learned to pick at their foods before they leave their native lands, they much prefer the attention that hand-feeding gives them. Therefore, the babies do not let the importer know that they can eat of their own accord. They demand hand-feeding, and they get it.

Actually, the handfeeding procedure is necessary at first. It gives the importer the opportunity of giving each bird a close inspection for condition and health, and it makes the transition period easier for the birds.

When the authors receive a new shipment of mynahs, they follow a set routine. During the inspection, each bird is given a precautionary aureomycin tablet compounded for birds, and a pet vitamin pill which also contains minerals. Because the new arrival is anxious for the attention and for food from a human's fingers, there is complete cooperation. The bird gladly gulps these pills down.

As soon as the bird is inspected, it is placed near food and water while waiting for the inspection of the others. As much as food, the new arrival wants a bath to clean off sticky feathers caused by the close confinement. By the time the initial inspection has been completed, most birds have bathed and are splashing water all over the place. A bit of preening follows while the writers observe the behavior.

A bird not feeling well will be reluctant to bathe and preen. Any who show reluctance are put in a hospital cage for a period of intensive care. Usually after two days, they can rejoin the others.

After the bathing and preening, the birds are fed by hand. The first few feedings approximate as closely as possible the foods the birds received in Thailand with several additions. An immediate switch to mynah pellets is not fully successful because the young birds will not take enough of them to maintain proper nutrition.

The food is varied. Cooked brown rice is used as a base with generous additions of a powdered vitamin-mineral supplement for

Young mynahs in an acclimation flight. These are Greater India Hill mynahs and Coletos from the Philippines. Because of their immaturity, the plumage is lacking in gloss.

pets. The first day, hard boiled eggs (cooked at least twenty minutes for easy digestibility) are added. During the day and evening each bird receives four handfeedings and will consume half an egg in the mixture. Mynah meal and canned dog food or horse meat are also added in small amounts at first and gradually increased.

The next day the eggs are omitted, and ground red chili peppers are added to the rice and supplement. To replace the native greens to which the birds are accustomed, the writers add chopped water cress and spinach. Drinking water contains a B-complex vitamin mixture now available for pets. This compound has rapid health restorative powers and improves appetite. The latter hardly needs improving, but the compound is nevertheless beneficial.

Between meals the birds are encouraged to pick out foods from food dishes. Thawed frozen peas and carrots are sprinkled on top of the rice mixture along with mynah pellets. The birds pick at these foods right from the beginning, but the intake is not enough to allow discontinuing the handfeeding for several days longer. Every group of mynahs is a little different, and time required for the transition period varies. They learn more quickly in groups than when kept alone.

At the beginning of each handfeeding, each bird is offered a few mynah pellets which they gladly accept because it comes from fingers. Each day a brewers yeast tablet is given to each bird. If not accepted, the tablet is pushed down into the crop which is a simple task because of the great gaping mouths and complete tameness. After a few days, they swallow them of their own volition. Brewers yeast is an additional food supplement especially high in natural B-complex vitamins. At one feeding each day, a pet vitamin capsule is given to each bird. There is no need to force these pills. They always seem to like them; possibly because they are small and bright red.

After the third day, all effects of the long trip have vanished. One of the handfeedings is discontinued and a fresh dish of food is put down at the feeding time instead. Within a few moments the birds are sampling the foods themselves, and they eat their first full meal on their own since they arrived.

Rice and the additives are gradually diminished and the proportion of mynah meal and pellets are increased. Fruit is gradually added; and usually in a week, the birds are onto a simple diet and are ready for sale. They are eating enough so as not to require more handfeeding even though they still appreciate it. Their ages at this stage average seven weeks. It is necessary to spray birds, cages, and aviaries each day during acclimation to eradicate any lice which may have accompanied the birds on the incoming journey.

For a few weeks, the diet should be diced fruits, raw meat, and mynah meal mixed in one dish and mynah pellets in another. The new pet owner can retain all the tameness and improve upon it by offering the pellets and bits of fruit from the fingers at frequent intervals. The authors recommend that their customers continue feeding one brewers yeast tablet and one vitamin tablet each day until one bottle of each is used (one hundred days). Many customers continue with the vitaman tablets as a regular and permanent part of the diet, and the birds thoroughly enjoy the extra.

With this importation routine, complicated though it is, the birds develop excellent dietary habits; and the transition or acclimation period is free from upsets. More or less, this is the usual acclimation procedure for many importers. However, this is the first time the authors know of that the information about the red peppers for the birds from Thailand has appeared in print. This is not just an extraneous additive, by the way. The birds are used to the peppers, and the dietary transition period is more successfully accomplished by including them.

When youngsters first arrive from overseas, the writers stuff the wide gaping mouths with vitamin pills, brewers yeast tablets, a precautionary antibiotic, and a few mynah pellets in addition to the foods to which they are still accustomed. As they become full of food, the beaks close; and the birds become a little obstinate about mynah pellets until they become hungry. After a few handfeedings, they gladly accept mynah pellets of their own accord.

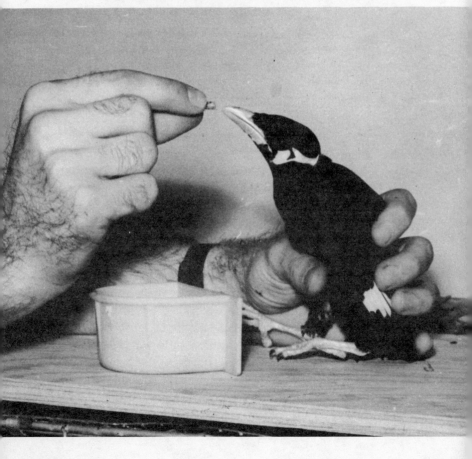

Chapter 4
Diet

With the manufacture of mynah pellets, the big problem of the mynah bird as a pet has been solved. Mynah pellets comprise a total nutrition in one single unit, and they may be used with confidence either as the total diet, or as a major source of the diet with only a few additions.

Mynah pellets are composed of just the right nutritional elements including a protein content of not less than twenty-five percent. They also contain a wide variety of dehydrated fruits and these too are very beneficial. The dehydrated fruits in most brands of pellets are apples, bananas, apricots, peaches, raisins, and dates. The mineral and vitamin contents are notably high, and they are easily digested because there are no heavy oils.

Mynah meal has the same nutritious formula as mynah pellets, but it is ground into meal rather than formed into pellets. Most mynahs learn to eat the pellets very quickly and prefer them to the meal. The meal is usually more acceptable when moistened with water. Too much water causes a sloppy texture. Add just enough water to make a fluffy texture.

Pellets can be fed dry or moistened, but it is a relatively simple task to teach your bird to eat them dry. There is little point in going to the additional trouble of moistening the pellets and then having to discard uneaten portions each day. Many people insist that their birds refuse to eat the pellets unless they are moistened, but this is merely an entrenched habit that can be changed by gradually reducing the moisture.

Mynahs have loose, sloppy droppings. Mynah pellets, more than any other combinations of foods, give firmness to the droppings. The greater firmness of the droppings indicates a state of better health. Many people feel that loose droppings indicate diarrhea; and, in most birds, this is correct. With mynahs and other softbilled birds, loose droppings are natural; but the soft foods which are often fed in captivity cause greater looseness than is advisable.

Many people feel that mynah pellets alone are a monotonous diet for their pet birds, and they want to know what else they can feed. Usually they go too far afield for treats, and end up causing harm to their pets. Extras, wisely selected, can be nourishing and interesting for the bird; and they can be helpful in maintaining tameness if most of them are offered by hand.

Limit the extras to fruits, ground raw meat, and peanut butter. The recommended fruits are apple, orange, and raisins soaked overnight in water. Raw meat must not contain very much fat. The best type to use is available for dogs and cats in pet shops. Both horse meat and beef are satisfactory. Hamburger is not good because it contains too much fat. In pet shops, the fat in beef for pets is usually held at fifteen percent. Horse meat fat is usually held at five percent. Hamburger, as most housewives know, may have up to fifty percent fat.

Peanut butter is a very nourishing food, and the peanut oil is easily digestible. Plumage becomes very glossy with peanut butter. Not all mynahs eat peanut butter, but most will quickly learn. It is perhaps not as easy to feed as the fruits and meat; but, if you plan to add any extras to the diet, this should be one of them.

The addition of fruits and meat will require more frequent cage cleaning because the droppings will contain more liquid, and the perches will become sticky because the bird will clean its beak on them. All of the additions should be limited because the bird may prefer the extras to the pellets. Cutting down on the pellets yields an improper diet. Before long serious deficiencies could lead to severe problems.

Before mynah pellets became available, feeding these birds was complicated and messy. The pellet foods are available in most areas now and should be used in place of the former diet.

In the event that mynah pellets are not available in your area, here is an alternative diet which is not too much trouble to prepare. As a base, use dry dog meal. Add just enough water to soak into a fluffy mixture. Add a powdered vitamin-mineral supplement such as is usually given to dogs and cats. If the directions do not state amounts for birds, add a little less than the recommended dosage for a very small kitten. To this mixture add diced apples, oranges, soaked raisins, and other fruits in season in a ratio of approximately one-half the total bulk of the dog meal. Then add about one teaspoonful of raw meat per cup of food. Mix well so that the bird does not pick out certain items and leave the rest. Some people add cooked brown rice to this mixture.

Dog meal in pellet form was successfully fed before the mynah pellets became available. The birds quickly learned to eat the pellets in dry form. In this instance, the fruit, meat, and vitamin-mineral supplement were mixed in a separate dish.

There are many other total diet mixtures possible, but they all become too complicated for the owner of a pet bird. One diet lists nine ingredients, and this formula is still deficient in several respects. When some of the more important ingredients are omitted the pet bird becomes more of a problem than a joy. Mynahs cannot, as stated in one book, "survive on about any kind of food available in the average home." In fact, such advice, if followed, will cause many problems in a very short time.

The problems with the two alternative diets mentioned above are the dangers from dietary imbalance and the need for greater frequency of cage cleaning. These diets are too soft, and droppings are always too loose. Moreover, mynahs do not very often select wisely when they are offered a variety of foods. The old theory that a bird will select the best items for a balanced diet if offered a wide variety of foods is a myth. Natural or acquired instincts for such a high degree of selectivity do not develop in baby mynahs because they are hand fed by humans on totally foreign foods before they are old enough to leave the nest. If the texture or color of a food appeals to a mynah, or if it is offered by a hand, the bird is likely to be interested. It can as easily develop a fondness for harmful foods as it can for nourishing foods.

The easiest and safest diet is the first diet mentioned in this chapter. Any extras, it must be emphasized again, should be limited to prevent dietary imbalances.

Mynahs should have food before them at all times because they eat small amounts frequently rather than large meals at specified times. Food should never be allowed to sour or to become moldy. Molds are particularly dangerous.

LIMITATIONS, AND WHAT NOT TO FEED

Never feed seeds of any kind. Mynahs have totally different requirements from seed eating birds. They are not equipped with a gizzard to grind seeds.

Most cooked foods are dangerous. Many birds show great excitement when human meals are served, and it is quite a temptation to offer "just a little" scrambled eggs and bacon. The cooking oils and

Here is the basic diet — Mynah meal, supplemented by the gresh fruit treats your bird will enjoy, and thrive on.

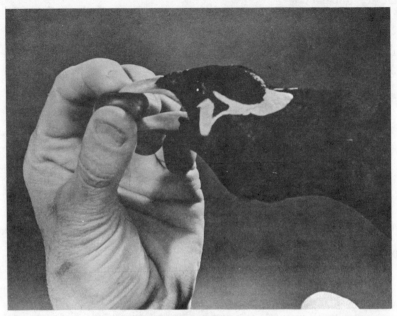

Treats which your mynah will like are better if they are offered from your hand in order to strengthen the companionship between yourself and the bird.

greases create many problems. They are in themselves extremely difficult to digest, and there are many instances recorded where frequent or more or less continued feeding of such tidbits have coated the mynah bird's intestines so much that food absorption became severely impeded.

Milk is a very harsh food for most birds including mynahs. It is not necessary and cannot be recommended. If you feel that you must give milk, at least use canned evaporated milk.

Potatoes and even spaghetti, oddly enough, have been recommended in books and articles in the past. They serve no useful part in any mynah diet. Potatoes and spaghetti are too filling, too fattening, and too short in food value. For large collections of softbilled birds, some aviculturists include cooked sweet potatoes as a small portion of the diet; but this is not a valid addition here. A caged household pet does not get as much exercise as an aviary bird and must not be allowed to get fat.

Grapes in season or soaked raisins at any time are excellent treats for a mynah. This type of treat is much safer and usually more nourishing than offering foods cooked for humans which can be very harmful.

Children are too frequently tempted to share their sweets with family pets much to the detriment of any and all pets including mynahs. Do not feed candies, cookies, cake, or other "treats" such as potato chips, salted nuts, or anything of this nature.

Some good food items must be limited. Bananas are fine, but they are fattening. Also, because most mynahs like bananas, they may want to eat more banana than anything else; and, if that is allowed, the diet goes out of balance. Orange is nourishing and greatly preferred by most mynahs, but it has an acid content which can be a little harsh in excessive quantities.

Chapter 5

Taming the Mynah

The industry supplying Greater India Hill Mynahs is so well organized and so efficient that an untame mynah rarely ever reaches this country at least during the fledgling season. All the youngsters are completely tamed by the period of handfeeding, and so the only task in this area for the bird fancier is to maintain the tameness.

A bird between four and six months of age can easily be retamed if the tameness is lost; but, as the bird gets older, recapturing the tameness becomes more and more difficult. A total retraining process becomes necessary with these birds if the owner wishes a tame bird.

As important as is the talking ability of the mynah, the authors would emphasize the virtues of the mynah as a tame pet. Few mynahs ever really show affection as do so many members of the parrot family, but tame mynahs are very friendly and gladly accept all the attention they are given. Also, they are highly inquisitive and intelligent to a degree that almost transcends the value of any outward show of affection.

Youngsters start to lose their tameness as soon as they become self-feeding. The loss is slow for some time and even slower if the birds are isolated. Dealers usually handfeed their birds longer than is necessary just to maintain the bond between bird and human.

If you buy your bird during the fledgling season, it is tame. To retain the tameness and develop a friendly personality, all you have to do is to give it some personal attention every day at least for the first few weeks. The type of personal attention is important.

Never tease your bird. It can become totally unreliable as a pet as a result of improper handling. You may not realize how subtle movements or handling will influence your bird. Don't pick up your bird bodily. This is especially antagonizing. Let your bird hop onto your hand and move around of its own accord while you are developing your companionship. When the bird is about to hop onto your fingers you must never withdraw your hand. This is a subtle tease which soon develops animosity. If you offer treats from your fingers, never hold them back. Such quick changes as this are the worst forms of teasing, and your bird will soon learn to retaliate.

Anger is easily developed as a personality trait in mynahs, and their retaliation can be unpleasant. Mynahs attack with their beaks and claws. They bite and pound with their beaks, and can pierce skin with their strong grip and sharp claws.

Never punish a mynah bird because it will quickly learn to return the punishment. Slapping the bird or cage or shouting at it will not only destroy tameness but will also develop the retaliatory personality which at any time can result in seemingly unprovoked attacks. This can become a firmly entrenched and frequently explosive habit.

Mynahs have strong memories and associations. The longtime pet Sahib owned by the authors had the freedom of the enclosed "pet patio" at the Palos Verdes Bird Farm. He enjoyed greeting visitors by flying to their shoulders and saying hello, and the visitors responded with pleasure. Sahib was a very gentle bird, but he eventually took a dislike to boys with crewcut hair, apparently because he had been teased by one. He associated the teasing with the short hair, and before long he was landing on all crewcut heads instead of shoulders. He attacked by pulling hair and pounding with his beak. It took several months of confinement in an aviary before he ceased the attacks.

Confidence and companionship are easily established with a mynah. Gentle stroking and petting and softly rubbing the head feathers are very helpful, but patting is not recommended. In time your bird will become so confident that it will even lie upside down in the palm of your hand. This trick, playing dead, will be one of the few tricks your mynah will learn. Mynahs are not great ones for learning tricks; but they have probing, inquiring personalities which will provide you with endless entertainment if they are given enough freedom to develop these traits.

Tameness in a mynah is as enjoyable as its talking ability. Mynahs are never as affectionate as parrotlike birds, but they can be excellent pets.

Completely tame mynahs can be allowed to sit on your shoulders if they have developed no untrustworthy tendencies towards retaliation or attacks which could prove dangerous. Of course, there is always the problem of soilage from the droppings. A protective garment will help.

A young mynah which has begun to lose its tameness before being sold can easily be reclaimed with patience and gentleness. Avoid rapid movements which tend to frighten. All approaches and movements should be slow, deliberate, and calm. Offer treats such as fruits from fingers to gain the bird's confidence.

Offer a forefinger for the bird to climb upon. If the bird ignores the offering but remains calm, nudge it gently upon the chest. The natural tendency will be for the bird to climb upwards if nudged. All the time talk softly to the bird. The tameness will be reclaimed in a very few days with frequent contacts such as this. The best time for such a campaign is during the relatively inactive orientation period while the bird is becoming accustomed to a new cage, new surroundings, and new people. Usually, the absence of other birds makes taming easier.

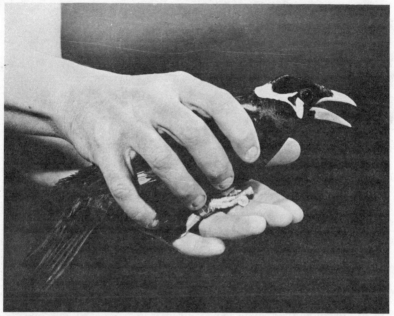

Most mynahs dislike being grasped this way and will voice their disapproval. Unless your mynah has been handled regularly in this manner from an early age, it will react as if this treatment is a punishment. It will learn to retaliate and could become unreliable as a pet.

If the bird panics repeatedly at these approaches, it should be given the total retraining routine. This rarely is necessary for a bird less than six or eight months old unless the bird has been badly mistreated. There are many birds which cannot be retrained, but all are worth the attempt. Some of those which cannot be retamed are good talkers. If they are untameable and non-talking, they are of little value as a pet and should be passed on to someone who is interested in breeding them.

The proper way to finger tame a mynah is to encourage it to hop onto your hand. To do this, nudge the chest gently with your forefinger. The natural response is to jump onto the finger. Repeat the process until the bird learns to respond without hesitation.

In the beginning of taming, the mynah may be put off balance by being nudged on the chest. After a few times, it will hop up without flapping its wings.

The retraining process for a difficult bird is slow and often seems to be unrewarding. A routine should be established and followed diligently and patiently. The bird in its cage should be placed in a quiet area away from bustling activity. The best time to try to tame your bird is during the evening when your bird is less alert. There will be less panic if the room is not brightly lighted. The approaches should be the same as described above. The bird's reactions will not show improvement quickly, and it will take many tries before the bird will hop onto your hand without considerable panic. At first, the main job will be to dispel fright caused by having your hand in the cage. This is perhaps the slowest part. Your soothing voice and offering of treats from fingers will be particularly helpful.

When the bird calms down enough after a time, take it out of the cage so there will not be the barrier of the bars between you and the bird. Here the routine regresses a bit because the bird must again become accustomed to a different set of circumstances. However, if the first steps have been accomplished, this one is certain to be successful.

Wing clipping may be favored by some trainers when this last stage is reached. When the wings are clipped, the bird is more dependent and therefore more easily tamed. The flight feathers may be clipped on one or both wings, or they may be stripped. Stripping is accomplished by cutting the webs off the flight feathers but the shafts are left intact. This is perhaps safer because there is less likelihood that the shafts will split down into the feather follicle which could mean ingrown feather problems.

Many Indian exporters in past years stripped the wings of youngsters during their handrearing stage, but the Thai exporters do not alter the wings in any way.

Young imported mynahs are hand reared and completely tame, but it takes proper handling to maintain the tameness into adulthood. This bird is having its head stroked and likes it.

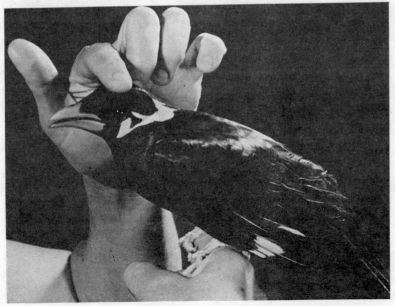

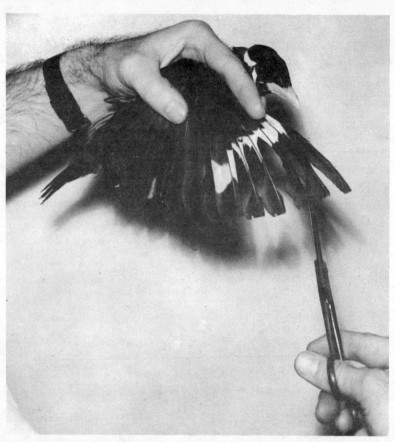

Instead of clipping wing feathers, many people prefer to "strip" the flights. This involves cutting the webs off the flight feathers leaving the shafts bare with spatulated tips.

Chapter 6
Talking

Mynah birds are amazingly adept at learning to speak. Both sexes are equally intelligent and learn just as rapidly. They mimic every human voice inflection and sound better than any other bird. They learn faster than parrots or parrakeets, and can master longer phrases even in the earlier stages of training. But don't expect your mynah bird to become self educated. Haphazard and half hearted training results in an endlessly tiresome repetition of a very limited vocabulary.

Mynahs are also known as whistlers, but it is a mistake to teach your bird to whistle. Mynahs learn to whistle more easily than they learn to talk; and they seem to enjoy whistling very much to the extent that they amplify their notes, often to deafening proportions. They also enjoy rearranging the sequences and tunes and frequently ignore their speech lessons. So teach your bird to talk instead of whistling to it.

A woman's or a child's voice is always better than a man's because of the resonance. A child usually lacks the perseverance to continue with the lessons; and so, for the first few words at least, a woman should be the teacher.

Enunciation should be very clear. This is one of the most important principles in proper training. The other principle is perseverance.

The tiresome part of teaching a mynah to talk is the first few words which require a longer period of time. Training records are available at pet shops to help during the initial stages. These provide a relief to the teacher's boredom and thereby help to insure the perseverance. Also, they are clearly enunciated.

After the first few words, training routines are far more enjoyable because the bird learns rapidly. Then the phrases can become more complicated, and all members of the family can join in the teaching. Frequent reviews of past learning are necessary so that the bird will retain all it has learned. Otherwise it might trade new words and phrases for old ones.

Mynahs are capable of developing amazing vocabularies of hundreds of words, phrases, and word combinations. Only in the very rarest of cases do the really diligent pet owners approach the total potentials of these highly intelligent birds. Most people become lax in their training regimen after the birds learn a few words and phrases. They become satisfied with a fraction of the bird's ability.

Failures in teaching young mynahs to talk can usually be traced to the teacher and should not be blamed on the bird. Either a high quality of training was lacking in such failures or the lessons were not consistent.

It is a mistake to teach your bird to whistle. The one with the wide open beak has obviously reached a very shrill state. The other one appears to be acting as a student. It will learn quickly. Whistling birds show less interest in talking.

Many people believe that a mynah learns up until a certain age and then stops. This is not true despite the fact that such statements have been in print in many different publications. Unfortunately, when mynah owners read such misleading statements from noted authorities, the statements usually tend to become facts only because the owners do not try to teach their birds any more.

Mynahs when properly and consistently trained will go right on learning as long as lessons are given. It is true that if lessons are discontinued for a long time and then started again, the interruption slows the learning process appreciably. Some individuals require so much additional effort that the task of resuming training is given up as hopeless. With most, however, perseverance will bring good results in a retraining program of a bird which already can talk.

Adult mynahs which have never been trained to talk, and which have lost their baby tameness can rarely be trained to speak.

The methods of teaching a baby mynah to talk are variable depending mainly on the owner rather than the bird. Lessons can be morning, afternoon, or evening whichever is most convenient for the owner; but they should be scheduled so that they can be consistently followed daily, with no interruptions.

Birds have their own periods of activity, and to use these periods for teaching would mean lack of attention and poor results. Mynahs have definite times for bathing, preening, and feeding. You must avoid these "activity" periods. If you prefer, you may work in a darkened room to minimize distraction.

Training periods should last about twenty minutes. If you stretch them very much longer than that, both you and the bird will lose interest. If you work for shorter periods, the impact of the lessons is greatly reduced; and your bird will require too many lessons to learn the first words. The period of initial learning can be greatly shortened by giving more than one lesson a day.

Start with a short, easy phrase or a double syllable word. Repeat the selected words again and again. Do not add other words. Pause a little between syllables or words. The bird will have a tendency to speak faster than you do when it learns. If you project your vocal lessons at a standard conversational pace, the bird will learn to speak too rapidly and will usually not quite master the sounds or inflections. Pause for a slightly longer period after each phrase so that the bird will not learn the sequence of repeating the phrase several times in rapid succession.

The first few words always require the greater number of lessons. Subsequent lessons are usually learned in much shorter time. The first lessons may have to be repeated several weeks before the bird masters them. Many young mynahs learn their first lesson in two weeks, but this is perhaps unusual and must be credited to the diligence of the teacher who is probably giving extra lessons.

If the first learning takes a long time, the teacher should evaluate the methods of instruction being used and should perhaps change tactics in order to produce greater effectiveness.

With effective teaching methods, the bird will learn new words and phrases in fewer lessons. Eventually it will learn in just a few lessons; and a few well-trained birds will pick up new words in a single day.

There are many reports of birds picking up a new word after hearing it just once. This is quite possible. The reason for such unusually rapid learning is that the bird's attention may be particularly attracted to the sound possibly because it has a different inflection or is spoken in a different voice or is pronounced with strong emphasis. If your bird develops such a talent you should guard against anyone who might inadvertently teach it embarrassing words or phrases. Swear words, for instance, are easily picked up by birds because they are pronounced with strong emphasis and a certain amount of vehemence. Moreover, they are short words. Birds learn such words because of these principles, and not because they are mischievous.

In the beginning, the student mynah, when it first starts to speak, will not enunciate clearly. There is a development period during which the speaking voice emits garbled sounds which are different from its ordinary bird sounds. When enunciation does occur, there may be errors or omissions. This period shows rapid progress; and, for the teacher, it is stimulating enough to warrant extra lesson periods which help to speed the entire process. Mynahs are particularly receptive to training for several months following this stage.

The range of a mynah's voice is quite extensive. Mynahs can speak in many different inflections, some of which may be developed without training. They speak also in different voices, high pitched, low pitched, and medium ranges. Unlike most parrots, the low pitched voice ranges of mynahs are clear and perfectly audible if the teacher has enunciated clearly. They do not assume a guttural sound as do most parrots who imitate men's voices. For variety, the bird may incorporate several different voice pitches in a conversational attempt. This occurs only in well-trained birds.

Some people teach their mynahs to sing. Others forget and lapse into whistling the tunes instead of singing. At the beginning of this chapter, the authors advised against whistling because the birds tend to ignore their speech lessons and spend their time whistling. Many whistling mynahs also turn up the volume on their whistling so that it becomes unbearable. From this point, it is only a short step to shrieking.

Mynahs learn to talk or to imitate other sounds quickly. They are usually very alert during their lessons.

Mynahs, because of their talent for mimicry, are attracted by other sounds as well as speech and whistling. They easily learn to cough and often learn to imitate the sounds of animals, squeaks, buzzers, horns, and other noises frequently heard in or around their environment. Some of these sounds are amusing.

CONDITIONED RESPONSES AND ASSOCIATION RESPONSES

Mynahs are more clever with conditioned responses than other birds. Many parrots are also very good, but mynahs more easily respond to this training technique.

The association technique can start after a dozen or so words have been mastered. By this time, the bird will already be connecting phrases, rearranging sequences, and sometimes interpolating extraneous words into the phraseology.

Conditioned responses are merely eliciting certain responses from certain actions or words. Suppose you want to teach your bird to say "Just fine, thank you" in response to your question "How are you today?"

To do this, your lesson period must become more rigid and should not vary until the response has become firmly entrenched. It would be most effective if the lesson could be held early in the morning when you first see the bird. If another time is necessary, an effective method would be to cover the cage with a dark cloth for a period of half an hour to an hour before the lesson begins. This will help to insure seclusion and a cessation of other activity which could be distracting.

As you uncover the cage or approach for the first time in the morning, say "Just fine, thank you." Never say anything else during these lessons except these words. Repeat them over and over again as in the regular lessons. When the bird learns to repeat the phrase, it will already have gained part of the conditioned response. However, you must continue with the lesson until it becomes established that the bird automatically answers "Just fine, thank you," because you approach the cage or uncover it.

When this becomes fully established, you approach or uncover the cage with the question "How are you today?" Then you must transfer the training so that when you ask the question, you will automatically get the answer. The training transfer is assured when the question gets the correct response at intervals other than the regular lesson periods. If you overdo the training, the bird could easily learn to ask the question as well as to give the answer. If this happens, some of the charm is lost.

Other conditioned responses can be taught with similar techniques, but each setting should be a little different because the first morning

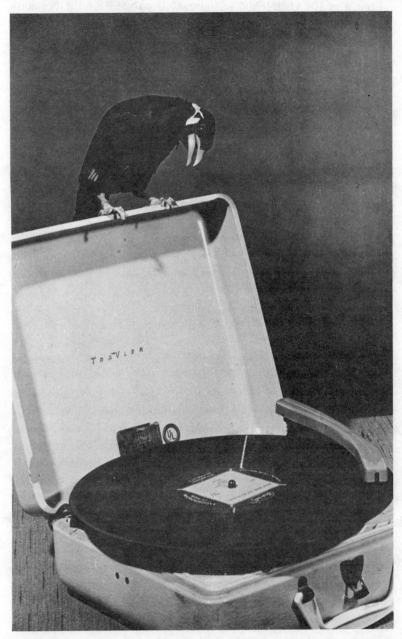

Training records are available at pet shops to relieve the tiresome perseverance needed in teaching the first few words which require much more time than later words and phrases.

approach or the uncovering has already been used for the previous conditioned response. To try to change the response to a given set of circumstances such as the early morning approach or the uncovering, results in confusion and slower training.

Eventually, the bird will mix up and rearrange its responses to some extent; but the complications and rearrangements can also be entertaining. The accomplishment in establishing conditioned responses is a rewarding experience.

RETRAINING

If your bird has learned to whistle or shriek or to be otherwise noisy and you want to eliminate these headstrong characteristics, you can also utilize the conditioned response technique in sort of a reverse situation.

Never try to punish your bird, or slap the cage, or shout at it, in order to break bad habits. The least you could do with your own temper tantrums is to teach the bird to shout back at you, and it is a well-known fact that these birds can be very stubborn. You could more easily instill a terrorized panic whenever you approach the cage. This would destroy all the bird's tameness and a good share of its vocabulary as well. Moreover, what vocabulary it would retain would be punctuated by shrieks of terror it has learned during punishment.

To break bad habits, you must act quickly but calmly. As soon as your bird starts on a noise-making spree, put it in total darkness by covering the cage with a heavy black cloth. You could also move cage and bird into a darkened room. The important part of this retraining technique is to act quickly as soon as the bird starts becoming noisy. It must learn to associate the noise with a darkened environment; this it will not like during its waking hours. If you consistently wait until the noise has continued for fifteen minutes, the chances that the bird will associate its noise-making with unwanted darkness will be greatly reduced. The sudden darkened environment may have to be repeated for weeks before the bird learns not to make noise, but this is nevertheless an effective technique. The authors have never heard of another workable noise deterrent.

Chapter 7
Cages

Because of the great number of mynahs imported for the pet industry each year, the number of styles of cages suitable for mynahs has also increased. Most of the newer styles or adaptations of other styles have followed the trend towards lower prices and smaller sizes. This is unfortunate because many of the lower priced cages are, in the long run, the most expensive to own.

A mynah cage should have a good, heavy, long-lasting plated finish because it will require frequent cleaning. A poorly plated finish will quickly begin to rust. A good cage will outlast several cages of poorer quality, and it will be easier to clean.

There are, to date, no stainless steel mynah cages; but stainless steel would be the best metal to use. The cost of producing suitably-sized stainless steel cages is too high at present to offer much hope for the near future.

Chrome plating is the next best type of finish, and there are several good styles and brands of cages with high quality chromium platings. Electroplated finishes are also available in copper, brass, and silver coloring. These are also very good, and are nearly as rust resistant as are chrome finishes, if the method of plating is of a high quality. Nickel plating is also very satisfactory.

Painted cages, some of which are still available, are not satisfactory for mynahs. The paint chips off, and the metal quickly rusts.

The size should be as large as possible. An ideal cage on the market is twenty-three inches high, by twenty-three inches long by sixteen inches wide. This allows for two perches spaced far enough apart so

Mynah cages should be as roomy as possible and should have a high quality plated finish for long wear. Inferior plating finishes start to rust very quickly because of droppings, regular bathing, and frequent scrubbings.

that the bird can gain some exercise jumping back and forth. This is actually better than a parrot cage.

Large parrot cages are satisfactory in some respects. Modern parrot cages usually have good plated finishes. They do not have two perches, and so the birds are perhaps less inclined to exercise. However, many have swings which help in persuading them to be more active. Parrot perches are a little too large for mynahs. Moreover, parrot cages do not have splash guards to help contain droppings and splashing bath water within their own boundaries.

Most large mynah cages and the better parrot cages have deep slide-out bottom trays and grills near the bottom. These two features denote specialized designs to accommodate mynahs and other soft-billed birds. Litter can be placed in the deep pans to help absorb the droppings, and the grill prevents the bird from moving about in the droppings and soiling its plumage and feet.

Absorbent material in a tray is fine if a grill is provided to keep the bird from picking it up on bits of food which may fall from the feeding dish.

The authors have successfully used litter for cat pans in the bottom of mynah cages because of its absorbent nature. However, a report from a reliable source indicates that this practice could be hazardous to birds which swallow quantities of these hardened clay-like granules. This could happen inadvertently when the bird drops fruit into the litter and then proceeds to eat the fruit and the clay particles clinging to it. A wise precaution would be to use cat litter only in cages where the grill is raised far enough to prevent the bird's access to the floor of the cage.

Sawdust or shavings should not be used on the floor of a mynah cage. Both of these are dangerous because of small splinters which puncture the intestines of the bird.

If the grill is too close to the floor pan to allow the use of cat litter, papers in several thicknesses can be used instead. Paper is not absorbent and must be changed more often than cat litter. Odors can be controlled with deodorants available in pet shops.

The cage should receive a thorough cleaning at least once a week. This means removing the bird and soaking the cage in water and a mild cleaning agent to remove any hardened particles of foods or droppings. Rinse it thoroughly to remove cleaning agents. The tray should be cleaned every day, along with any other areas where soilage is concentrated.

The metal should be wiped dry after cleaning and bathing. This precaution will add years of use to your cage by curtailing the beginning of rust spots which quickly spread once they have started.

Perch care is very important. Several mynah problems begin with feet. Dirty perches cause the scales of the feet to become clogged with droppings and sticky foods. The birds clean their beaks on perches after eating fruits or soft, moist foods. The best method of cleaning perches is to scrape them lightly with a knife and then to go over them with a perch brush which is available at pet shops. The use of a perch brush prevents the perches from becoming hardened.

Scraping them clean with a knife gradually hardens the surface of perches to such a degree that callouses and other painful foot ailments could develop. Washing perches is safe only if two sets are available. Dampness from slow drying perches invites rheumatism and similar problems. If you have a spare set to use in the cage while the damp perches are drying, washing the perches as a regular part of the cleaning routine is satisfactory.

A good mynah cage has a grill to separate the bird from the droppings. It should also be deep enough so that a layer of absorbent cat litter can be spread over the bottom out of reach of the bird. High splash guards are also useful.

Housing your mynah in an indoor aviary is ideal if you have the space to build one. Nearly any size is adequate so long as the proportions give the bird room for exercise, and your cleaning chores are simple. Welded wire fabric is the easiest material to use in constructing an aviary because no framework is needed for an average indoor aviary.

If the bird is subject to easy panic, the tautness of welded wire may be hazardous. Aviary netting is more flexible and therefore a little safer than welded wire fabric, but it requires a framework.

The floor pan or bottom of the aviary, however you construct it, should be one that is easily cleaned. Perhaps one of the best ideas in constructing indoor aviaries is to have the aviary on legs with a wire grillwork of welded wire fabric at least a foot above the floor. In this way, the floor can easily be cleaned with little effort and no disturbance to the bird. The wire grill must be cleaned also but not as often as the floor.

Chapter 8
Breeding

Despite the fact that a great many mynahs have been imported during the past decade, there have been very few successful breedings in captivity. The few successful breedings which were recorded in the 1950's pointed out many unsuccessful attempts as well.

The problem at that time was improper diet. The basic mynah pellets were not then readily available. There were so many extras added that most diets ended up completely out of balance merely because the birds would select the wrong items. Though many eggs hatched, very few young ever reached the fledgling stage.

Now, more is known about diets of softbilled birds and the extras which are needed during the nesting periods; but mynahs are still rarely raised in captivity. Part of the reason for this somewhat odd state of affairs is the exceptional industry which supplies world markets with such fine handreared nestlings for pets.

Handreared youngsters of all types of birds, not just mynahs, experience interruptions in the orderly development of their natural instincts, many of which are of the nature best described as "inherited memories" and some of which are gradually acquired during early development. Handfeeding of youngsters can in many instances block breeding instincts or at least can cause errors in their early efforts. This theory has been held by the writers for several years. It may not be correct, but it is a well known fact that many tame birds are very poor breeders. There are notable exceptions with all types of birds to be sure, but the percentage of breeding failures among tame birds is unusually high even when the tameness has been discouraged

Sexing mynahs is difficult. In addition to the differences in wattles, males usually stand more erect and a little taller than females. However, stances can change quickly; and this "pair" in a few moments may show opposite poses. If these birds follow a reasonably consistent pattern of stances, the bird on the left may be assumed to be a male and the one on the right is female. The assumption may be made even though the wattles are not yet fully developed.

and the birds are put into spacious aviaries to condition them to breeding. Tame birds which have been tamed after weaning have far less of an interruption in their natural instincts; but nearly all mynahs in this country, whether still tame or not, have been handreared by natives in their countries of origin before shipment to this country.

Another reason for the lack of breeding success even though more is now known about diets is that most of the pets are considered too valuable to relegate to secluded aviaries, and the thought of despoiling a talented pet for a remote chance of raising youngsters does not appeal to very many people. The price of mynahs has also consistently become lower and lower in the last decade, and there is no real incentive for anyone to undertake the commercial breeding of Greater India Hill Mynahs. Importing is far more economical except for those additional varieties which are very seldom available.

Sexing mynah birds is not a particularly easy task. The length of the wattles is significant in adults; with males having considerably longer flaps on the nape. However, improper development or illness can cause changes in these flaps. During illness, these flaps can shrink appreciably. Age also makes a considerable difference. Males also have a bolder stance than females, and usually stand with their heads higher. Males are slightly larger. However, none of this is evident with youngsters.

Those who raise mynahs do so because of the challenge and the accomplishment. It is not a simple task. To set down a lot of rules invites a flood of exceptions, but there are a few suggestions which should help to bring about ideal conditions.

The aviary should be sizeable and, if possible, well planted with shrubs or small trees. The length should be at least twelve or fifteen feet, and the height should be not less than six feet. Eight feet or more would be far more desirable because it would allow for more freedom of movement for humans who must attend the aviary, with less disturbance for the birds. Width really does not matter much. Four or five feet in this direction is really quite sufficient.

Breeding mynahs should receive as much seclusion as possible. If this cannot be arranged, they should become accustomed to as much intrusion as possible so that they will not react unfavorably when someone not known to them approaches their aviary. Most male breeding mynahs become very aggressive towards anyone entering their aviary, even towards people with whom they have previously been friendly.

On the other hand, a pair of Coleto mynahs which the writers once owned went to nest on a large covered patio in which visitors and customers roamed in considerable numbers. The birds had become so accustomed to people that they paid no attention to the crowds. However, they resented the other birds and were merciless in attacking some of them.

Mynahs usually take a considerable amount of time to settle down in a breeding aviary before they begin to nest. Upheavals and re-arrangements can destroy all hopes for success. It is wise to select pairs as much in advance of the breeding season as is possible. They should be given an aviary to themselves. As in most softbilled breeding aviaries, running water is a great advantage. Mynahs love to bathe even more than do most softbills; and, with a fresh supply of water at all times, mynahs have a greater feeling of security.

Mynahs are very hardy birds; and, in southern California or areas of similar climates, they can be wintered outdoors in unheated aviaries if properly conditioned in the summer. In cold climates they should be given protection, and most people in cold areas keep mynahs in heated aviaries, or inside during the winter.

The diet for breeding mynahs is the same as for the pet mynah, with a slight variation. Live foods are usually more important. Pets usually pay very little attention to live foods; but, in trying to develop breeder mynahs, the resurgence of natural instincts is helped by the addition of as many live foods as possible, including young mice. The fast growing youngsters require enormous quantities of foods, and the high protein content is important. Raw ground beef or horse meat is also an important addition.

Mynah eggs compared to a penny. The nest is a rather loose affair.

All of the mynahs mentioned in this book follow the same procedures, and share the same requirements for breeding.

Mynahs accept a Cockatiel nestbox which averages nine by nine inches square by fifteen inches high with an entrance hole about three inches in diameter. The entrance perch should extend inside as well as outside the box.

Twigs and straw and even leaves are used in constructing the nest. The birds spend a great amount of time arranging and processing the materials. Nevertheless, the nest still is a loosely constructed and not altogether tidy affair.

Eggs are blue-green spotted with brown, and are quite large, considering the size of the bird. They are laid on succeeding days rather than alternate days, and so they hatch one day apart rather than every other day. Three eggs is an average clutch. The incubation period is two weeks with some birds taking a day or two longer. This short incubation period shows exceptionally rapid development. The female does most of the incubating and feeding of the chicks.

Young Mynahs a few days old. The pinfeathers on the wings are showing. So is the appetite.

The chicks grow rapidly. In a little over a week pinfeathers and wattled areas are already becoming noticeable. They start to show signs of leaving the nest at three weeks of age but usually do not leave until the fourth week. They start to eat by themselves at six weeks of age, but the weaning process is slow. Unless they are to be hand fed, they cannot be removed from their parents at this age.

Though the different species of mynahs are usually consistent in most habits, the age at which they start to breed is inconstant. The smaller species breed at earlier ages than do the Greater India Hill Mynahs. The latter species does not usually show good results until both birds are three years old.

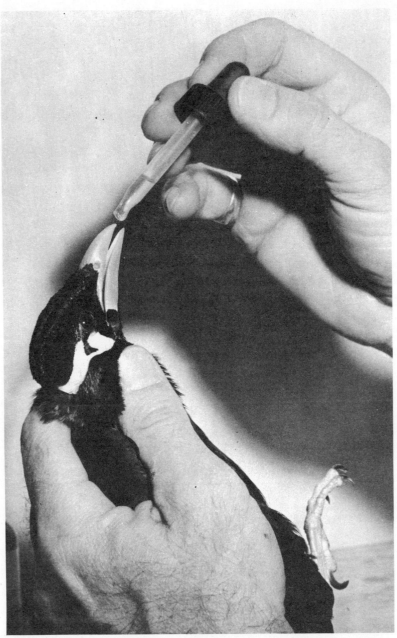

Medication with a medicine dropper is easy if you properly tamed your pet when it was young and healthy.

Chapter 9
Diseases and Cures

Mynahs are very hardy and long-lived birds. Ailments and diseases do not often occur except through neglect, or mistreatment, or improper diet.

There is no excuse for malnutrition or an unbalanced diet, and such a condition will not occur if you follow the chapter on diet. Precautions must be taken against letting the diet fall into even subtle imbalances. The chapter on diet should be reviewed every few months and compared with the diet you are giving your bird to be certain that it has not gradually slipped.

Symptoms of most illnesses are listlessness, loss of appetite, dull plumage, fluffed feathers, loss of color in the wattles, occasional shrinking of the wattles, and dull eyes.

CONVULSIONS

One of the most puzzling and most serious problems which occasionally affects mynahs is fits. The convulsions can be very severe and erratic in occurrence. Deaths have sometimes occurred, but injuries happen more often. There can be two causes. One cause is too much sunshine. The other is an out-of-balance diet. The immediate treatment is to remove the bird from its cage to prevent injury. A soft box will help. It is all right to wrap the bird in a cloth to help curtail the convulsion, but loose cloth or unsecured padding in a box or cage is dangerous because the stricken bird could become fatally entangled. Darkness sometimes helps, and a spray of cold water has been known to bring the bird out of its convulsion.

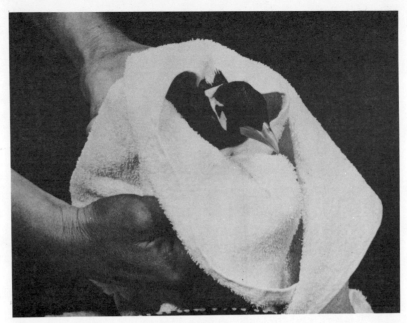

If your bird should ever become subject to convulsive fits, this is one way to prevent the bird from injuring itself. See the chapter on ailments to understand this rare but serious problem.

Warmth after the convulsion is the starting point for eliminating the cause. If the cause is improper diet, eliminate all extraneous foods. The bird should receive extra raw meat and mynah pellets, a vitamin-mineral supplement, and some fresh fruits, but nothing more. The minerals and meat are of prime importance in restoring the balance.

There is no build-up to ward off the effects of too much sun. A caged mynah should never be placed in the sun because it will have no opportunity to move into the shade as it would if it were housed in an outdoor aviary. Overexposure to sun has, in many instances, caused death. Convulsions are serious and the bird owner should consider them a strong warning signal.

FIRST AID
First aid should be the first stage in the treatment of nearly all illnesses. In many ailments, first aid is enough to bring about a full

recovery. When a bird does not feel well, its temperature usually drops. Instead of eating more food to help rebuild stamina and restore its naturally high temperature, the sick bird eats less and loses still more stamina.

The components of first aid are quite simple. Heat, about 80°F. day and night, is necessary to help maintain body temperature. A twenty-five watt light bulb placed just outside the cage will help. The cage should be covered on the top and all sides except the front. The bird will not be disturbed by the light at night. It will sleep often during the day and night. With the light burning at night the bird will be encouraged to eat more often. Life's lowest ebbs occur at night. Light and heat help to eliminate the natural low points.

Appetizers, generous and easily accessible food supplies, and a precautionary antibiotic or wonder drug are the other components of first aid. The antibiotic or wonder drug can be sulfamethazine or aureomycin, both of which are available at pet shops especially prepared for birds. Directions on the package should be followed carefully. Overuse of antibiotics can be harmful because they kill helpful bacteria as well as harmful germs and because they can permanently damage the organs of elimination. Antibiotics are excellent, but they should be used carefully.

Appetizers to add to drinking water for pets are not too well distributed as yet, but more and more pet shops are carrying them. Their main components are B-complex vitamins in liquid form. They are easily administered, and they work successfully to improve appetite.

Foods should be placed so that the bird will not be able to easily ignore them. They should be placed at different levels so that no matter where the bird perches food will be at hand.

During illness, foods may have to be changed to entice the bird's interest. Most of the battle of keeping a sick bird alive is to keep it eating as much as possible. To do this, offer more fruits, raw meats, and cooked diced carrots and peas.

One particularly helpful formula which the authors have used with many kinds of ill birds is 100% liquid. It is also effective with birds which refuse to eat during acclimation periods. Because of the higher temperatures recommended, most birds will drink more than they eat while they are ill. A liquid will therefore be more readily accepted. The ingredients used by the authors are noted for their easy digestibility as well as high nutritional value. Blend one table-spoon of honey, one tablespoon of peanut butter, and one tablespoon of Mellins Food with a little hot water and work until they are smoothly dissolved. Then add enough tap water to bring the total level up to one cup. Substitute this for regular drinking water. Appetizers and medicines can be safely added.

COLDS

Colds, most of which are caused by drafts, are very dangerous because they can go into severe secondary infections such as pneu-monia, asthma, and clogged sinuses. The birds do not readily cooper-ate with treatments of any kind. When they do not feel well, they lose appetite and refuse food as well as medicine. First aid is especially helpful, but it is not enough.

The severity of colds can vary considerably; but, in most instances, wheezing, difficulty in breathing, and nasal discharges are noticeable. Other symptoms are the standard symptoms for most illnesses.

This bedraggled bird is not ill, just wet from its bath. Just be sure it can dry off quickly, thoroughly before it takes a chill.

Administering pills may at times be necessary. To make this a simple task, the bird should become accustomed to pills while it is still young. The writers teach youngsters to accept vitamin pills at a very early age. After this, they usually quite readily accept brewers yeast or aureomycin. There is one inherent danger in this plan. The birds will also accept other small objects which could be very harmful.

An antibiotic or sulfa drug is mandatory. It will not completely clear up the cold, but it will help to prevent the more dangerous secondary symptoms, like pneumonia. The authors use both sulfamethazine and aureomycin prepared for birds. To use both together is satisfactory, provided directions are followed. Their usefulness overlaps to some extent, but both are effective against a greater number of offending organisms.

A cold remedy and a mild inhalant for birds help to dry up mucous and to prevent clogged sinuses. Asthma, pneumonia, and impacted sinuses are the three problems which follow unattended colds.

Asthma can cause a bird's death, but more often it is a chronic ailment which is very prolonged and difficult to treat. Laborious breathing, minimum endurance, and open mouthed wheezing are the most noticeable symptoms. Treatment often takes six months, but it is not a continuous treatment.

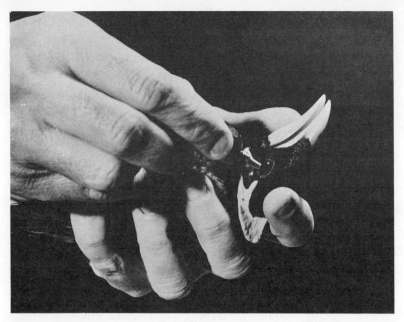

Eye problems are very rare. They usually are symptoms of more serious sinus complications. Clogged nostrils require frequent attention, and an eye medication must be administered often to facilitate normal drainage of tear ducts. The chapter on ailments outlines treatment for more complicated or severe cases.

Sinus disorders are usually easy to detect, and simple ones are easy to treat. Watery eyes and clogged nostrils are the initial symptoms. Cold remedies and inhalants work well with most of these problems. A more severe result not uncommon in mynahs is a sinus impaction which results in a large, rapidly growing nodule of hardened mucus above the eyes.

Preventing the impaction is easier than treating it. Inspect the nostrils frequently to be sure they are not clogged. A matchstick or blunt tipped similarly sized instrument can remove substances which cap the nostrils.

To remove a nodule of hardened mucus requires more careful handling. The authors inflict a small wound in the skin above the central area of the nodule. The resulting scab which develops in a very short time will attach itself to the mucus nodule. Gentle massage will break the scab and nodule loose, and the nodule can be removed through the opening of the wound. Further massage will ease the remaining impacted cheeselike material from the sinus passages. All the material must be removed or else the condition will quickly recur. In severe cases, the nodule may recur and need removing several times before the condition disappears.

FEATHER DISORDERS

Feather disorders rarely occur in mynahs. The moulting period, usually the last six weeks of every summer, is a natural method of replacing old feathers for new ones. Not all feathers are replaced, and no one area becomes totally bare during a normal moult.

Proper diet has erased the problem of bare spots or baldness which once occurred on a frequent basis. With the mynah pellet diet as

If eyedropper administration becomes necessary, this is not the safe way to do it. In the roof of the mouth is a slit which connects to the windpipe and lungs. In this position, the liquid will drain right into the opening slit. The bird should be held upright, and no more than two drops at a time should be administered.

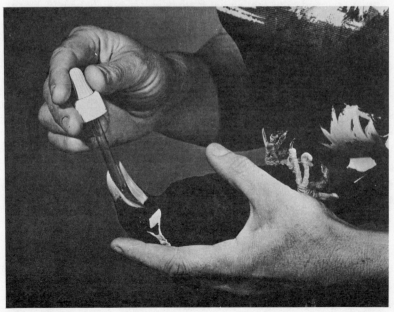

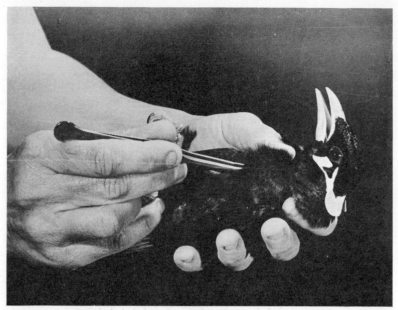

Ingrown feathers may be the result of skin injuries on the chest. Healing scabs cause irritations to the bird, and the bird prolongs the healing process by picking at the scabs. They should be softened by one of the several healing salves available at pet shops. Ingrown feathers must be removed after the injuries have been completely healed. Chest injuries occur during retraining procedures of adult birds which have lost their tameness. Clipped wings are necessary in this process, but the bird may suffer from heavy falls before it learns not to fly.

efficient as it is, no other food additions are required during the moulting period. Should feather problems arise, the addition of minerals and animal protein to the diet would be helpful until the problems are corrected. Feather replacements usually take up to six weeks to complete. The animal protein can be furnished through raw meat (horse or beef), and the minerals can be supplied by a powdered vitamin-mineral supplement prepared especially for pets.

Broken feathers may split down into the feather follicle which could result in imperfect replacements or ingrown feathers. The most frequent cause is wing feathers which have been clipped too short. Ingrown feathers are imprisoned by very thin skin. A slight slit with a razor blade will provide an opening with very little bleeding.

The imprisoned feather will usually have to be removed since it will not grow into a good strong useful feather. In removing the growing feather, there is a strong likelihood that bleeding will be profuse because developing feathers which are encased in a pinfeather sheath have a very high circulation of blood. Removing the entire pinfeather sheath is necessary to discourage bleeding.

To stop bleeding entirely, household hydrogen peroxide, monsel's salts, or a styptic pencil, can be applied to the treated area.

Mynahs have a strong grip, and tame birds must have the sharp tips of toenails removed occasionally if they are to be handled comfortably. Pet shops have nail trimmers for dogs which prevent the nails from shattering. Usually only the tips need to be removed.

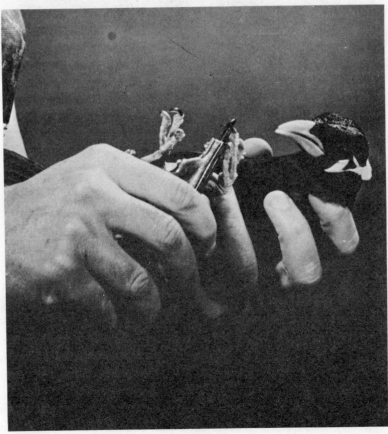

If it becomes necessary to pick up an adult mynah, this is the proper way to do it. The wings are restrained to prevent injury in the event of panic. Youngsters can be picked up very easily. They have no fear and enjoy the attention, but adults react differently unless they have been accustomed to frequent handling as a regular practice.

OTHER PROBLEMS

As long as the diet is correct and sensible precautions regarding general care are followed, there will be few other problems or ailments.

Clean, properly attended perches prevent foot problems; and very few mynahs need their toenails clipped as do many other types of birds. Beak trimming is necessary only if the bird has a malformation.

Mites rarely become a problem if both bird and cage receive frequent cleanings. Sprays for mites are available at pet shops if this need arises. Several feather sprays are also available at pet shops if they are needed.

Molds and sour crops occur only if food supplies become old or spoiled. Since mynah pellets have been available, the simplification of the diet has practically removed all of these problems. Food should not be allowed to remain in the cage for long priods, however. Bath water splashed on mynah pellets can produce molds after a time.

Shocks and heart attacks are usually brought about by sudden panic. Tame, well poised birds are rarely affected. Slight earthquakes such as are often felt in California do terrorize many birds including some mynahs. The main precaution is to prevent the bird from injuring itself if it flies into a wild panic against cage bars.

Diarrhea or constipation may occasionally occur with no symptoms of other disorders. Usually these two problems are in themselves symptoms of other diseases and are only secondary complications. Balanced diet is the best preventative measure. Should either con-

Care of legs and feet is relatively simple. Frequent bathing usually prevents scaliness, and toenails rarely grow too long unless the perches are too large. Pet shops have salves and ointments to help soften hardened scales for easy and natural shedding. If toenails are clipped too short, bleeding can be stopped by household peroxide, iron sulfate (monsel's salts), or a styptic pencil. In severe instances, cauterizing the wound may be necessary. This can be accomplished by quickly touching the tip of a lighted cigarette to the bleeding toenail.

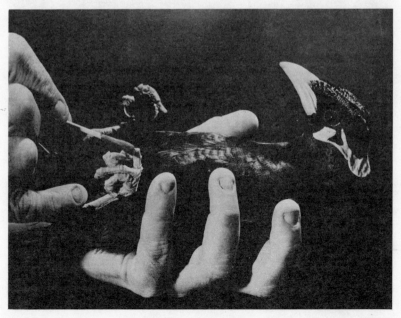

dition occur with no other accompanying ailments, the simple treatment is the same for both in most instances. A good laxative will clean out the digestive tract. The writers use one tablespoonful of black strap molasses in a pint of distilled water. This is given instead of water for two days. If diarrhea should return after this treatment, the writers then turn to a commerical diarrhea remedy which pet shops carry. The commercial products have a soothing, coating effect on inflamed membranes in the digestive tract. The writers use the black strap molasses treatment first because it gives quickly absorbed food value as well as relief in most cases from both problems. It must be remembered that both diarrhea and constipation produce results similar in appearance. The droppings from constipation have a very liquid nature because the feces are held back. What appears to be diarrhea may, in many birds, actually be constipation.

Chapter 10

Other Mynahs

The family of mynahs and starlings is very large, and it includes many exceptionally beautiful birds which are easily kept in aviculture. Many of the more than one hundred species are various forms of starlings; and most of these are prohibited entry into the United States. Unfortunately, the laws are variable from state to state and apparently variable in interpretation on the federal level as well.

There is a very important reason for restrictions. The Common Starling, as everyone now knows, was an unfortunate importation. This bird was deliberately established to help control harmful insects. Its incredible adaptability has made it a pest in many parts of the world. Other members of the family could also be pests in many parts of the world if introduced. One example is the Common Mynah (*Acridotheres tristis*) which is abundant in many introduced areas, notably Hawaii. It would be wrong to extend many of these species. In most instances, the introductions were deliberate because these birds consume enormous quantities of insects. They are even now beneficial in this respect, but they crowd out most of the other birds in their introduced areas. They reproduce great numbers of youngsters, and do not have their natural enemies to check population explosions.

Unfortunately, the restrictions include too many species. As mentioned above, the laws are variable. California at the moment of writing excludes all members of the family except those of the genus *Gracula*. Other genera are acceptable in many other states.

Common Mynah (Importation to U. S. prohibited). Drawing by G. W. Noreen.

Pied Mynah (Importation to U. S. prohibited). Drawing by G. W. Noreen.

G. r. peninsularis. Drawing by G. W. Noreen.

Coleto Mynah. Drawing by G. W. Noreen.

Pagoda Mynah (Importation to U. S. prohibited). Drawing by G. W. Noreen.

Gold Crested Mynah. Drawing by G. W. Noreen.

At least two genera and all their species should be prohibited: *Acridotheres* and *Sturnus*. A few members of these two genera are the ones which have caused the problems. Not all of the members of this family would adapt easily to foreign environments, and many are so rare and expensive that adequate safeguards would be given against any accidental escapes. The popular names "mynah" and "starling" are often used interchangeably for many species in the two offending genera, and nearly all birds bearing those popular names are considered as importation risks.

There are several fine species of mynahs and starlings occasionally available to bird fanciers. Most are better known as aviary birds than as cage birds or talking pets. Some will learn to talk if given the same training outlined in this book and if started while they are young enough. None are as talented in this respect as those of the genus *Gracula*. Several are noted as talking pets in their homelands.

Many mynahs are not available to worldwide bird markets because of their remote habitats or because they do not occur in countries where there are export markets. These are omitted from this book. Also, since this book is about mynahs, starlings will be omitted.

The care is the same as for the Greater India Hill Mynahs, but most of these are less robust than the regular talking mynahs. The acclimation period is usually longer; and, since most of these will be adults, the transfer to our diets is a little more difficult. Youngsters always adapt better than adults. Nevertheless, most mynahs are among the most easily acclimated of all birds.

COLETO MYNAH (*Sarcops calvus* with three subspecies)

The Coleto Mynah is from the Philippines with one subspecies in the nearby Sulu Islands. It rarely is available even though it is not a particularly expensive species. It is not a beautiful bird, but it does have a very unusual appearance. The length totals eleven inches from the tip of the one-inch beak to the tip of the four and one-half inch tail.

The body and head are smaller than those of the Greater India Hill Mynah, but the slender tail is longer and more rounded on the end. The head has a severe bare skin area which gives the impression of a naked skull. This wattle skin covers the head back to the hind-crown and down to the lower beak area excluding the throat. A feathered narrow black line runs down the center of the head and

The Coleto Mynah from the Philippines is an unusual species which is rarely available. The chalky bare head skin can blush to pink. The back of the neck and rump are shiny silver.

across a very narrow forehead. All the bare skin area is surrounded by black with only a narrow border at the back of the head. The beak is also black.

A large crescent of shiny silver across the back of the neck extends down to the upper mantle. Another large area of shiny silvery-gray starts at the middle of the back and becomes more intense on the rump and the small feathers covering the base of the tail. The same color extends onto the lower side areas. Youngsters have silvery-gray shades with less gloss; and adults show more silver than gray, always shiny.

The rest of the bird is entirely black. The black in adults is glossy in all areas except the undertail coverts, but youngsters lack the gloss which gradually appears starting with the fifth or sixth month of age. The feet and legs are a blackish-flesh color. Both sexes are alike in appearance as well as talent.

The bare skin or wattle flesh on the head is variable in coloring depending upon the bird's mood or temperament. The average shade is chalky-flesh, but it frequently blushes to deep pink. If the bird does not feel well, all trace of pink leaves the skin; and a faint trace of blue occasionally shows in the white.

Coleto mynahs have a ringing bell-like call note. They are frequently kept as caged talking pets in the Philippines. They must be started as youngsters if they are to learn to talk and to be tame.

Java Hill Mynah (with missing tail) is larger than the Malayan Greater Hill Mynah (on the left). Note also the different wattle patterns. The Malayan Greater Hills resemble the Indian except that they have smaller slimmer bodies and legs, and a finer black line in the center of the skin patch near the eye.

The European Starling is another cousin of the Mynah. Intelligent and agressive, it has invaded North America and all but driven the Bluebird from inhabited areas.

The Purple Glossy Starling, like the European Starling, is intelligent and aggressive. Neither has the ability to mimic like the Mynah, but they are kept as cagebirds in Europe.

Rothschild's Mynah **(Leucospar rothschildi)** is one of the most beautiful but it does not have a reputation for talking. Photo from Am. Mus. Nat. History.

GOLD CRESTED MYNAH (*Ampeliceps coronatus* sometimes erroneously identified as *Mino coronatus*)

The Gold Crested Mynah comes from India, Burma, Thailand, Cambodia, Laos, Vietnam, and northern Malaysia. It is reasonably common in Thailand and usually reaches worldwide bird markets from export centers in Bangkok. This species only recently became available to bird fanciers, and is still quite rare. It is more likely to be considered a beautiful aviary bird rather than a caged pet. It is not known for any talking ability as yet, but it is possible that it could learn to talk a little if started at an early age. Youngsters, however, are far less attractive than adults because they usually lack the bright golden yellow coloring on the head.

The Gold Crested is a little over eight inches in total length. The body is stocky; and the tail is broad, short, and squared. Both sexes are alike. Bare wattle flesh in a yellowish shade surrounds the eyes in an extensive area. The beak is orange-horn in color. The shape and proportions are the same as in the Greater India Hill Mynah.

Bright and glossy golden yellow covers a large area including the chin and throat and on top of the head from the forehead to the lower nape. The area behind the eyes and sides of the neck remains black. There is a short bristly crest on the forehead. A large area of yellow covers the central area of the flight feathers which in the Greater India Hill Mynah is white. The female has a shorter crest and less extensive yellow on the throat.

All the remaining plumage is black with glossy green and blue reflections. Feet and legs are yellowish-orange.

ROTHSCHILD'S MYNAH (*Leucopsar rothschildi*)

The rare Rothschild's Mynah is native only to Bali. It is one of the most beautiful of all mynahs and is highly coveted by bird fanciers.

This species is about ten inches long with pleasant proportions and a heavy body. Most of the coloring is snow white with bold black accents on the tip of the tail and on the ends of the flight feathers. A large blue flesh mask surrounds the eyes and tapers to a tip on the sides of the neck. The thick beak appears to be short because the feathered forehead extends far to the front. The upper mandible appears to be only half as long as the lower mandible. The beak is mostly bluish-gray with dull yellowish-horn in an extensive area at the tip. The feet and legs are soft bluish-gray.

Black Winged Mynah (**Gracupica melanoptera melanoptera**) helps emphasize the diversity in color and form to be found within the Mynahs. Photo from Am. Mus. Nat. History.

The crowning glory of this species is a thick, graceful crest composed of many slender, supple white feathers. The crest area starts at the forward part of the extended forehead where the feathers are short and extends back to the nape. The crest feathers become progressively longer back to the crown. All those on the hindcrown and upper nape are particularly long and graceful extending backwards almost to the lower nape.

PROHIBITED MYNAHS

Other mynahs available to worldwide aviculture belong to the two genera *Sturnus* and *Acridotheres*. These are specifically denied entry to the United States. Bird fanciers would be interested in some of them as aviary birds if they were available. Many youngsters become tame pets, but none will ever be known as good talkers. There are still other species of mynahs in other genera, but they do not occur in established collecting areas.

INDEX